Warren Holden

Many Moods

Warren Holden

Many Moods

ISBN/EAN: 9783743303430

Manufactured in Europe, USA, Canada, Australia, Japa

Cover: Foto ©ninafisch / pixelio.de

Manufactured and distributed by brebook publishing software (www.brebook.com)

Warren Holden

Many Moods

MANY MOODS

BY

WARREN HOLDEN.

PHILADELPHIA:
PRESS OF J. B. LIPPINCOTT COMPANY.
1895.

COPYRIGHT, 1894,
BY
WARREN HOLDEN.

CONTENTS.

LIFE'S CHANGING PHASES.

	PAGE
Memory	9
Love at Sight	10
Love's Silent Ministry	11
The Beautiful, the True	12
Illusions	13
Innocence	14
Evolution of the Yacht	15
The Tiger Hunter	16
The Sportsman	17
Driving	18
Adventure	19
Solitude	20
The Whaleman	21
The Mule-spinner	22
Ambition	23

CONTENTS.

	PAGE
Disarmament	24
Patriotism	25
Aristocracy	26
Diogenes	27
The Medici	28
Harmony	29
Stability	30
Repose	31
The Inventor	32
The Engineer	33
Poetry	34
Art	35
Music	36
Fiction	37
Love Immortal	38
Home	39

EARLY VERSES.

Wandering Alone	43
The Orphan	47
Niagara	53
Dramatic Sketch	60

CONTENTS.

AFTER-THOUGHTS.

	PAGE
O tongue-tied love, too slow, too poor of speech	67
Parted! and must I see the face no more	68
Though veiled from outward sight thou art more near	69
Not hers the gift to trace from hidden start	70
Too late! Too late! If only he had known	71
It seemed the flowers of her garden knew	72
If Mary or Martha were her proper name	73
From the rank harvest-fields of bitter woe	74
It is the quiet Sabbath's twilight eve	75
Still tugging at the heart from yon dim shore	76
Give me realities, the sceptic said	77
Bereavement finds no solace but to weep	78
Said Prudence: Let us win the wealth to-day	79
The things you fancy real may be so	80
Patient thou waitest for us there above	81
How dull and slow we are to apprehend	82
How fondly when a fellow Christian dies	83
The heart still longs whate'er the lips may say	84
Show me the way to heaven, a spirit prayed	85
Beyond the border, where the wicked cease	86
Day after day she filled her wonted place	87

	PAGE
Another peaceful holy-day is o'er	88
As shadows lengthen from the setting sun	89
On the world's stage what though the *rôle* of pain	90
Days, weeks, months, years are gliding swiftly by	91
To pass away when full of honored years	92
No more shall vain regret indulge the wrong	93
"There is no death," though the wan spectre, fear	94

THROUGH FOURSCORE'S SPECTACLES.

The Boat-race—(Intercollegiate)	97
The Meet	98
Gossip	99
Sham Aristocracy—(Family, Wealth, Sanctity)	100
The Practical Man	101
The Great Money Lender	102
Modern Travel	103
The Bully	104
The Dude	105
Fiction	106
Pessimism	107
Criticism	108

LIFE'S CHANGING PHASES.

MEMORY.

Gray memory, boon companion this cold night,
  While travellers belated face the bleak
  North winds that, round us howling, entrance seek,
  We hug the cosey fireside blazing bright.

On by-gone years thy presence sheds a light.
  Of half-forgotten scenes 'tis thine to speak,
  Recalling passages that blanch the cheek,
  Or waken laughter, mischief-loving sprite.

Rehearse the tale of boyhood's escapades;
  The wild adventures of more reckless youth;
  The mad ambitions ruling manhood's prime

That laughs to scorn contentment's peaceful shades;
  But dwell we most on friendship's loyal truth,
  And love, the good supreme, outlasting time.

LOVE AT SIGHT.

A WILD and wayward child of liberty,
 His only law immediate delight;
 No bird was more erratic in its flight,
 No prairie steed obeyed a will more free.

A single glance decides his destiny
 From eyes that speak in smiles of liquid light,
 Awaking looks responsive that unite
 Two hearts in one for all eternity.

What earlier charms had touched the unripe breast
 With that o'erwhelming passion flood are blent
 To swell its tide to a life-lasting stream.

Seen through the rosy haze of love's young dream,
 Nature looks gay in bridal garments dressed,
 And every creature smiles with sweet content.

LOVE'S SILENT MINISTRY.

How many a modest face reflects the sheen
   Of perfect love! No blazing trump of fame
   Needs loudly tell of love's immortal flame.
It sheds a glory silent and serene.

Be sure thou keep the faultless mirror clean;
   Nor seek by tinsel ornament to claim
   Undue regard for its surrounding frame.
Beauty when unadorned is fairest seen.

Favored of God and well beloved of men,
   Sweet human face, thine office is divine:
   To image goodness all unconsciously.

Beneath love's crowning halo hid from ken,
   Be thou content with borrowed light to shine
   For others' weal, though none remember thee.

THE BEAUTIFUL, THE TRUE.

Love's first begotten, beauty, must be true.
   A child takes beauty's hand, a trusted guide:
   With charmed expectance wending by her side,
We humbly worship while we fondly woo.

With frowning face stern duty bids: "Thus do,"
   And, puffed up with her own self-righteous pride,
   Makes it her chief delight to check and chide.
What youth could frankly love the homely shrew?

The sceptic intellect, discreet and slow,
   Would have us wait for proofs before we dare
Enjoy the gifts the gracious heavens bestow.

But the warm heart is instant to declare
   The truth it doth intuitively know;
Through faith's swift logic doubt dissolves in air.

ILLUSIONS.

In life's bright morning when the heart was young
   And all the wealth of love obeyed its will,
   How far off were the cares and fears that kill;
How like wild flowers spontaneous friendships sprung.

Nor when by cruel wrong the heart was stung,
   And shrank alarmed at the discordant thrill,
   Could it believe that friendship meant it ill,
But to its loved ideal faithful clung.

"Illusions,"—croaks wise age—"akin to youth,
   "On foolish fancies of the nursery fed,
   "Scarce out of leading-strings as yet, forsooth."

Then would I might remain a child misled,
   And never come to know the heartless truth,
   Those dear illusions still my daily bread.

INNOCENCE.

WATCH the spontaneous motions of a child
   With love's discerning eye, and you may trace
   The simple beauty, the unstudied grace
   Of native innocence still undefiled.

Unbidden fancies, bird-like roving wild,
   In frolic freedom every moment chase
   Each other o'er the quick responsive face.
   Care smoothes her brow, by sudden charm beguiled.

Unconscious vehicle of love divine,
   Thou goest heedless of thy precious freight,
   Spilling its jewels all along thy path.

Would heaven that changeless childhood might be thine,
   Too soon, alas! through some untoward fate,
   Thou mayst become a vessel filled with wrath.

EVOLUTION OF THE YACHT.

The wayward boy's ideal is to rove
  The boundless, pathless mystery of the sea,
  From irksome discipline and duty free,
And subject only to the law of love.

Loose morals leave wild fancy room to move,
  As the winds change, from trade to piracy.
  His bent derives from Viking ancestry,
Who dared all deaths their manhood to approve.

As boyhood's mountain billows slow subside,
  And hurricanes are lulled to summer breeze,
  The rover's bark evolves the pleasure yacht.

Over the rolling waters safe we glide,
  Fair-weather sailors cruising at our ease,
  The dangers of the raging sea forgot.

THE TIGER HUNTER.

THE jungle harbors hungry beasts of prey
  That nightly hunt their game; nor turn aside
  For human hunter, whose disdainful pride
Joins battle, savager the while than they.

What fierce delight,—unawed Bengal at bay,—
  In single combat calmly to abide
  The issue skill and courage must decide!
It is a game for manliest men to play.

Wonderful being whose loves and passions range
  Throughout the gamut of created life!—
  Æolian harp of Spontaneity.

With change of wind at once thy tune doth change
  From joy to grief, from peace to deadly strife;
  Thou inverse counterpart of Deity.

THE SPORTSMAN.

WHILE yet the dew is sparkling on the field,
  Soon quaffed for morning draught by the early sun,
  The cheerful sportsman, with his dog and gun,
Hastens to harvest what the woods may yield.

The unsuspicious birds, whose fate is sealed,
  Make no attempt that cruel fate to shun,
  Singing sweet matins any heart had won
Save hardened Nimrod's to soft pity steeled.

At night, returning home with well-filled pouch,
  The hunter needs must glory in his art
  If he would sleep in peace upon his couch;

Since he hath caused the dearest mates to part,
  And many a fledgling must unsheltered crouch;
  And many a nest conceal an aching heart.

DRIVING.

An open road, clear sky and bracing air;
   A clean-limbed, spirited, and well-matched team;
   'Tis an exhilarating joy supreme
To hold the reins and guide the dashing pair.

The varied beauties of the landscape fair,
   Like a swift-moving panorama, seem
   Successive changes of a vivid dream
That crowds a lifetime in one vision rare.

Swift thought flies back to Rome's trained charioteer
   Striving for victory in the reckless race.
   And as he turns the goal, the deafening cheer

Of the mad multitude, whose hearts keep pace
   With the mad driver, bursts upon the ear
   Like Pandemonium broke loose from its place.

ADVENTURE.

Adieu to the dull, changeless round of home.
    In the fresh strength of life's exultant prime
    Rove we the boundless Ocean; hark the chime
Of its four winds while ploughing through its foam!

Or dreary deserts let us choose to roam,
    And dismal, untrod forests hoar with time.
    Nor let our venturous footsteps fear to climb
The loftiest Alp, and scale its ice-glazed dome.

With waning years we claim the chimney nook;
    And gathering simple children round our knee,
    Rehearse the perils that befell our youth.

Or write the marvellous story in a book
    To let the home-abiding million see
    How far mere fiction falls below the truth.

SOLITUDE.

CONFUSION of the city's Babel noise,
   Vain struggle betwixt poverty and pride,
   Far from your mean distractions let me hide,
   Equally wearied with your cares and joys.

Freed from society's absorbing toys,
   Amid the solemn desert let me bide;
   Or climbing the lone mountain's arduous side,
   In solitude regain lost equipoise.

Ye venerable stars that still pursue
   Yon paths, by human passion undisturbed,
   Admit me to your silent fellowship,

That I may learn the selfhood to subdue,
   And, vulgar demonstration duly curbed,
   Many worship with a finger on the lip.

THE WHALEMAN.

"There she blows!" "Where away?" "On the lea
    bow."
"Man the boats—lower—ship oars," and off we go.
A race to win the prize we madly row,
As through the surging waves our way we plow.

Unship the oars; use noiseless paddles now,
    Lest we alarm the monster moving slow;
Until the harpooner his iron throw.
Small chance to miss does that wide mark allow.

Off shoots leviathan swift as a dart.
    How the line spins while flying from its coil!
To follow in his wake is now our part,

Till he's quite spent beneath his freight of oil.
    Then the mate's lance, well aimed, may reach his heart,
And sixty barrels shall reward our toil.

THE MULE-SPINNER.

TRIPPING beside the homely spinning-wheel,
   Content with methods of the olden school,
   And shy of new inventions, happy fool,
The rustic maiden plies her task with zeal.

But the world moves, and all the impulse feel.
   Our blithesome lassie, turned a factory tool,
   Races all day beside the spinning-mule,
Like dancing dervish in his dizzy reel.

At night shamed-faced she steals to near saloon.
   The hated stimulant is only sought
   To keep the breaking heart awhile in tune.

Thus day by day is wasting strength o'erwrought,
   Until the victim sinks at last in swoon
Beneath the wheels of modern Juggernaut.

AMBITION.

Born to command, Ambition knows no law
    But dictates of an arbitrary will,
    Nor halts at any means that may fulfil
His aim to conquer and to overcome.

So he but win the popular huzza,
    And with his name the trump of fame sound shrill,
    What recks he though a sea of blood he spill,
And though the undying worm his vitals gnaw.

Thus having gained a cold and barren height
    Above the reach of human sympathy,
    In loveless isolation he must dwell.

Or banished from the outraged nations' sight
    To some lone prison island of the sea,
    There let him rue his self-created hell.

DISARMAMENT.

The powers stand armed expectant of the fight.
    If one adds strength, the rest must quick increase.
    A word, a gesture, even, may release
The fiend of war to ravage and to blight.

Claiming to battle only for the right,
    They ask what means would make all war to cease,
    That 'neath the fig-tree and the vine of peace
Each might pursue at ease his own delight.

Near-sighted self sees but the selfish side,
    Nor dreams what wealth united strength could win;
    But hoards a private heap and tries to hide.

Oh for a touch divine to prove our kin,
    Make all in each and each in all confide,
    And bid God's Kingdom on the earth begin.

PATRIOTISM.

To fight for despots is not patriot zeal.
 The soldiers of an arbitrary power
 Are slaves, unless they hope to haste the hour
 Shall usher in true freedom's commonweal.

Yet liberty makes but a vain appeal
 Where rival factions hungrily devour
 The very germ of freedom's tender flower,
 While grief distracts the bosoms of the leal,

Let heart and hand, let brain and brawn unite
 In self-devotion to the common cause
 Of right for all and privilege for none.

Then were a country for which men could fight,
 Though met each step by death's devouring jaws,—
 Fight till the sacred height of truth were won.

ARISTOCRACY.

THE worthy sons of noble ancestry
    Alert to keep their scutcheons ever bright,
    Their heirlooms, virtues, gems of purest light;
    Their cleanly lives from blot and blemish free;

These friends of man, unbribed by any fee,
    Who freely give their service in the fight
    To baffle wrong and reënforce the right,
    Deserve the name of aristocracy.

Whether they shine as ministers of state,
    Conspicuous leaders in the highest place;
    Or, whether in the closet they create

The thoughts that move mankind; with equal grace
    They serve their age, like angels sent by fate,
    The benefactors of the human race.

DIOGENES.

Diogenes sat basking in the sun,
   Content to gaze on nature's quiet face;
   He coveted no monarch's lofty place;
   For fear or favor would he bow to none.

Great Alexander's course had scarce begun,
   Ere he assumed the patron's pert grimace.
   "Tell me what boon, of my imperial grace,
   I shall bestow that may thy wish outrun."

"I only beg that thou wilt stand aside,
   And not obstruct my share of heaven's light,"
   So answered sturdy manhood, head erect.

When will heaven's stewards learn to curb their pride,
   Too prone to meddle with man's private right,
   And tempt the poor to barter self-respect?

THE MEDICI.

The Medici wrought nobly long ago
   As world-wide merchant-princes of their age,
   Who cherished art with royal patronage.
   Down the long stream of time their praises flow.

Witness the grand career of Angelo,
   Whose works remain a nation's heritage,—
   Statues whose fame invite a pilgrimage;
   Saint Peter's dome that greets the sun's first glow.

Our *modern* Medici may lead the van
   Of patrons of a higher form of art,
   The shapely moulding of the immortal mind.

Out of the rough-hewn mass of formless man,
   Concealing beauties native to the heart,
   Are sculptured masterpieces of our kind.

HARMONY.

O HUMAN heart, thou harp of many strings,
   Responsive to the tender touch of love,
   Thy tones seem echoes of the choirs above,
And nature's every voice in concord sings.

But when rash passion its rude finger flings
   Across the living chords, they quickly prove
   That lurking discord lies in wait to move
Man's darker moods to angry mutterings.

With ill-trained skill we try our several parts
   In eager effort to express the soul.
   The great world-soul derides our futile arts.

Oh for a master hand whose firm control
   Might harmonize the music of our hearts,
   And into one grand chorus blend the whole.

STABILITY.

Man's law is change. His works last but a day.
   His architecture crumbles into dust.
   Engines that served their turn are gone to rust.
   To modern schemes time-honored use gives way.

Can art and science boast a longer sway?
   Do human rights and laws continue just?
   Even hoary creeds, perchance, betray their trust.
   Where can we look for freedom from decay?

Look to the sky with its eternal blue;
   The tireless sun that daily does his part;
   The stars to their fixed courses ever true;

Mountain and sea, all forms of nature's art;
   And sunset hour the same yet ever new.
   These treasures never fail the trusting heart.

REPOSE.

With noiseless step unruffled nature goes,
 With ease her children reach their proper goal,
 As seasons alternate and planets roll.
 With quiet power all real progress flows.

The tempest's rage, the earthquake's frantic throes,
 The haste and wrath of the impatient soul,
 Alike betray disease beyond control.
 But healthy action springs from deep repose.

Restless ambition seems awhile to thrive,
 Heaping up riches which can never buy
 The peace of mind that underlies pure joy.

But heirs of nature need not madly strive
 For wants that moderate labor can supply,
 While placid thoughts their tranquil minds employ.

THE INVENTOR.

What change the new creator brings about!
Embodying thought in lever, screw, and wheel,
He quickens enterprise to burning zeal,
And puts the clans of idleness to rout.

Attacking every citadel of doubt,
   This bold intruder hastens to reveal
   What ignorance and prejudice conceal,
And lets mute nature's well-kept secrets out.

As he unfolds new wonders, everywhere
   Behold dumb forces in blind Samson's place,
   Emancipating every human slave.

Our modern Hercules, ordained to bear
   The burdens that before had crushed the race,
   Still plies his task to succor and to save.

THE ENGINEER.

Giants and genii, in creation's prime,
   Amused credulity with marvellous feats
   Of engineering which, though naked cheats,
Were true predictions of the coming time.

They taught our daring engineer to climb
   Up to the wonder-working demons' seats,
   And wield their weapons with a skill that beats
His masters, with results indeed sublime.

A flimsy web he sees the spider throw.
   Straight o'er the gulf an iron bridge he flings,
   And, like a mole, a thoroughfare he bores

For rapid transit's unobstructed flow.
   Soon shall you see him plying mighty wings
   In his swift flight to far-off foreign shores.

POETRY.

Deem not the poet's happy world a mere
    Ideal scene, an unsubstantial dream;
    The music of his rhythm an artful scheme
To captivate a too fastidious ear.

Is love an empty dream? and are the dear
    Delights of pictured peace that make the theme
    Of all his musings never what they seem,
Losing their glamour when the light grows clear?

The inner world of mind and heart alone
    Endureth. Outer show may change each day
    In fickle fashion's quick kaleidoscope;

But poets' promises broadcast are sown,
    Prolific seeds whose plenteous harvest may
    O'erfill the measure of prophetic hope.

ART.

The artist would immortalize his theme;
  Whether it be the charm of beauty's smile
  That from the living canvas shall beguile
  Successive generations like a dream;

Or whether he would stay the dazzling beam
  Of sunshine that illumines yonder isle;
  Or paint the patriot orator's grand style
  When freedom's holy passion reigns supreme.

See the endurance pictured on that cross,
  Where death assails the Life that cannot die,—
  Immortal guidepost to the promised land.

Bless the memorial art that saves from loss
  The soul's expression when its aims are high,
  Proving the heart's best promise nigh at hand.

MUSIC.

WHAT saith the voice of music to the soul,
   Now speaking low in sweet persuasive tone,
   Like a young lover pleading for his own;
Now choked with tears, refusing all control?

Led by the siren where the sad waves roll,
   We share humanity's unending moan.
   Or rapt to heights of bliss before unknown,
Hope finds new life, her broken pledge made whole.

A common language, native to the heart,
   It needs no skilled interpreter to spell
   Its meaning, plain as speech of mating birds.

Language of love, all innocent of art,
   Thine only is the happy gift to tell
   Of joys and griefs beyond the power of words.

FICTION.

The Sun as limner paints the actual face,
   Whether its charms attract or faults repel.
   Impartial truth biography must tell,
If it exalt a name or prove it base.

But Art, the sphere of harmony and grace,
   Rejects whatever weakens beauty's spell.
   So fiction's hero, fashioned to excel,
Of dull realities scarce shows a trace.

With all the spoils of time at its command,—
   The brave and free, the generous, the great,
   The wise and good, since history began,—

Unfettered fancy culls, with dainty hand,
   The rarest forms wherewith it may create
   A perfect model, the ideal man.

LOVE IMMORTAL.

WHILE homeward faring at the close of day,
    A strain of far-off music greets the ear.
    In the faint tones the heart will choose to hear
    Its own dreams echoed, making glad the way.

So toward life's close a note of some old lay
    Has power to bring the scenes of childhood near,
    With all the joys to early friendship dear.
    Alas! that love should ever know decay.

Love cannot die! Its first-fruits may seem lost.
    Too eager youth may rue a hasty choice;
    And hearts must ache ere trial make them strong.

But love forever lives. Though sadly crossed
    At times, though often choked with tears, its voice
    Shall yet be heard in hymeneal song.

HOME.

Each morning man goes forth with serious face
   To meet the duties of his daily round,
   Whether in narrow circle he be bound
To manual labor's dusty commonplace;

Or whether loftier ambitions chase
   The rarer game that haunts the higher ground.
   If mid the marts of trade his place be found,
Or if he bear heaven's messages of grace.

Calm evening, gentle shepherd, to the fold
   Leads back the weary one to welcome rest,
   Beneath a lowly roof or lordly dome.

Shut to the door. Exclude the world's heart-cold
   Regard. Let not to-morrow's care molest.
   For a brief while enjoy the peace of home.

EARLY VERSES.

WANDERING ALONE.

'Tis a joy of my life to be wandering alone
  Through the paths of the forest when Summer hath
    flown
  And Autumn's feet rustle,—unvexed by the throng,
  To attend to the stillness revealing the song
Of many-toned nature,—the fingering breeze
  Attuning æolian harps in the trees;
  The choral of insects; the orchestral birds;
  The brooklet whose babbling doth counterfeit words;
The far-distant waterfall's lingering drone.
  Let no whisper be breathed while I listen alone;
  Intruding society, break not the charm
With your clamorous laughter and notes of alarm;
  The prodigal passions have sunk into rest:
  Dear angel of Peace, for a while be my guest.

O welcome, ye woodlands, in garments that vie
  With the many-hued robe of the sunsetting sky,
  When the year, at its evening departure, like day,
  Takes its way o'er the hill-tops in Tartan array.
Let me join thee, contemplative Eve, in thy round
  Over mountain and valley to earth's furthest bound,
  Surveying new landscapes by twilight subdued,
  Till the tone of each spot hath my spirit imbued.
I'll return with the morrow, my own chosen Grove,
  Oh, believe not that Eve could seduce me to rove.
  Your novitiate Druid aspiring to be,
  I frequent your seclusions a vowed devotee;
Meandering your labyrinth led by the brook,
  While we search for the secrets that hide in each
    nook
  Of your hermitage. Stay, sweet companion, we drink
At this fountain that gushes through rocks at thy
    brink,
  And repose 'neath yon grotto with moss overgrown.
  Thus wandering with thee is not living alone.

To be winding along by the sinuous shore,
    From each new point of view the same scene to explore;
    Multitudinous billows that crowd to the strand
    To contribute their mite to the numberless sand;
In unending succession wave following wave
    Lay their life at your feet and retire to their grave;
    Far-off voices, commingling in unison, roar
    Evermore, evermore, from Eternity's shore.
'Tis a sobering joy. thus to wander alone,
    While there comes o'er the waters that lingering moan
    Whose monotone murmurs in sympathy's ear
    Of humanity's miseries mournful to hear.
Meditation unbosoms her burdensome woes,
    And to pitying heaven our weariness shows.
    Breath of Life! breathe an influence calming the storm
    That relentlessly preys on the mariner's form.
Fount of Hope! let thine oasis timely appear
    To the pilgrim who faints mid the desert of fear.
    Light of Love! be the smile of thy countenance shown
    To the outcast who wanders in darkness alone.

Over mountains remote let me wander alone,
  There is life in each tree, there's a voice in each stone;
  A sweeter companionship solitude knows,
  And a sympathy nearer than friendship bestows.
Let the midnight of winter o'erspread its dark veil,
  Loose the winds to outpour their disconsolate wail,
  And with ruin to mark where they trample a path:
  Though I tremble with awe, yet I relish their wrath.
Ye vehement Tempests, give ear to my vow,
  Record it, ye Lightnings, on heaven's dark brow;
  Proclaim it, ye Thunders as dreadful ye roll;
  I love you, I love you, ye friends of my soul!
Ye share every feeling, acknowledge my wrong,
  Rejoice in my joy, and disdain not my song.
  Indulged in each mood, like the heir to a throne,
  He that dwelleth with nature is never alone.

THE ORPHAN.

The dream of my childhood is fled,
  The charm that so sweetly beguiled
Is dissolved, and the brightness it shed
  Is quenched in the gloom of this wild.

I thought in those innocent dreams
  The world was a garden of bliss,—
Full of flowers and enlivened with streams,
  Where love could be bought for a kiss.

There fancy her guests would invite
  Life's banquet and dance to begin;
And we revelled with purest delight
  Till a grim-visaged spectre stalked in.

Forth he stretches his palsying hand
    And but touches fair promise to blight;
    The enchanter but waves his weird wand,
    Where but now all was day all is night.

I awoke to a morning of cloud;
    My fairy-built fabrics had passed,
    And hopes, that late flourished so proud,
    Had been crushed by the tramp of the blast.

Farewell to my infancy's home;
    Bereft of each tenderer tie,
    Life's desert an exile I roam,
    And fain from myself I would fly.

Ah, hard is the orphan's lone fate,
    To the world's cruel mercies resigned;
    On him love and home shut their gate;
    He's an outcast, the sport of each wind.

How I long for that home once so dear
  Where, begirt with life's holiest bond,
  I had nothing to wish or to fear,
  Beloved by a mother so fond.

Oh, had I the wings of a sigh,
  How soon I'd behold her again;
  How soon, at her home in the sky,
  In reunion forget every pain.

While shrouded and coffined she lay,
  I thought the strange slumber would end,
  Till I saw, with heart-rending dismay,
  Earth yearning to swallow my friend.

O my mother, in anguish I cried,
  For what have they torn thee from me?
  Would heaven thou never hadst died,
  Or that I might be buried with thee.

Blighted hope cast its buds in her grave
  One by one with the clods as they fell;
  Naught survived but the cypress to wave
  O'er the spot, my sad story to tell.

Oft I sat 'neath its desolate shade
  And watered its roots with my tears;
  Musing still on the griefs it displayed,
  As still with its growth grew my fears.

Like the harp that is played by the air,
  Which so sweetly responds to the breeze,
  But shrieks like a soul in despair,
  If winter's cold hand on it seize;

It is thus with the harp of the heart.
  While love breathes along its soft strings,
  A music more sweet they impart
  Than the song which the nightingale sings.

O'er those heart-strings to harmony tuned,
  Let but sorrow's rude fingers be flung,
And discord bewails at the wound,
  While each nerve of the soul is unstrung.

Forsaken by man and by God,
  Unarmed for mortality's strife,
Thus weary and faint as I trod
  The thorn-planted pathway of life,

Seemed to issue this voice from the tomb:
  "My forlorn one, my child, come to me;
Death is kind; Oh, regret not thy doom,
  My bosom thy pillow shall be."

Dear mother, thy voice glads mine ears;
  Runs thine orphan to meet thy embrace;
In thy bosom to bury his tears,
  And never again miss thy face.

Adieu to this world's gloomy vale,
 I'll make her cold grave my death-bed.
Stingless death, vanquished grave, bid ye hail!
There is rest, there is peace with the dead.

NIAGARA.

A PILGRIM to thy shrine, Niagara,
I heard afar thy sullen voice, deep-mouthed
Like mutterings of some fateful oracle.
Still as the fascination drew me on,
The stunning uproar swelled upon my ear,
With such continuous and o'erwhelming power,
As drowned all thought or feeling rational.
Pale fear took hold on me and shook my heart,
But with returning confidence, returns
A loftier mood, fit for such lofty theme;
When mingling gradual with my listening thoughts
Softens its terrors, till at length it comes
Like music—music that hath meaning in it.
Ye intermeddling passions, peace. Be still,
Intruding thought, and let my inmost soul
Drink in the strain that pours melodious
From yonder organ-loft of nature's fane.

Inspiring music, oft in dreams, methinks,
Thy solemn tones have come to me betimes,
As angels ministrant of mild reproof,
Though awe attend thy deep, stern eloquence.
Then have I wept and promised to repent;
And waking I have cherished the dread peal,
Till it became a well-remembered voice
To soothe and cheer me in my lonely hours.
We are not strangers. Oft have we communed
The whiles thou didst discourse of things eternal.
E'en now, as in a waking dream, thou hold'st
Fast locked my senses that they dare not stir,
Lest they disturb the awful charm that reigns
In the deep silence which thou dost impose;
And I should lose one note of that high song
Which human discord cannot interrupt.

O sacred minstrelsy, enchant me still;
And mingle with earth's thousand other hymns
To magnify the skill that pitched thy pipes

To loftiest symphonies. Servant of God,
The sermon thou dost preach hath reached my heart.
The seed which thou dost scatter with thy spray,
Shall spring to full fruition in my soul,
And shall bring forth the blessed fruits of peace.
For though thy rostrum be the naked rock,
And the vexed elements fit audience
Of thy rude ministry, thou'rt yet to me
True harbinger of peace. Thy voice, long heard,
Becomes familiar as a mother's voice,
That whispers peace; and I could lay me down
Amid thy din and calmly fall asleep,
E'en as a child soothed by a lullaby.

What apparition from the spirit land
Dilates my startled sense with grand surprise!
I saw thee in the distance like a cloud,
But not intently could peruse thy form.
The eye was then subservient to the ear,
That would admit no partner in her joys,

Thus the rich melody possessed me whole.
But now on near approach, and looking up,
As wakened from a dream, I *see*—I see
What laboring words would vainly strive to paint.

A flood thou seemest, coming in thy might
Again to overwhelm the guilty world,
(As taught in parable of Noe's time,)
And, for a moment, weak in faith, we doubt
The promise, till we look upon thy brow
Where God hath set His rainbow for a token.

Hail, bow of promise, never more shall flood
Of falsehood's turbid waters drown the earth
In one wide deluge, suffocating good.
Hail, bow of promise, from henceforth the floods
Shall symbol only plenteousness of truth,
Whose fountains, erewhile sealed, now broken up,
Do leap forth joyous in their liberty,
And spread their healing waters everywhere;

And purge away the accumulated dust
That hath disguised the real forms of things,
And show them as they are, or good or ill.

Oh ever haunt my mind, thou vision bright,
Impress thine image on my glowing brain
With spiritual seal indelible;
That frequent fancy may contemplate thee,
Eternity upon time's canvas drawn.
There art thou as thou hast been from of old,
In undiminished beauty and full strength,
Retaining all the freshness of thy youth.
Time groweth old; thy twin-born rocks decay,
And crumbling piecemeal drop into their graves,
Dug by thy feet, receding with slow step,
Whose each enduring track marks centuries.
But thou remainest, yesterday, to-day,
Perhaps forevermore the same, unchanged,
Worthy thine origin, and His fit type.
On that majestic forehead calmness dwells

While at thy feet tempest and whirlpool rage,
A vast abyss of power beyond control.
Call it Omnipotence in miniature,
If such resemblance traced offend Him not,
Who did perhaps conceive the high design
As a remembrancer to thoughtless man.

Stupendous fountain, I could worship thee,
But that I know thy greater Fountain head
The Wellspring of all life, whence we came out,
And whither we return.

Perennial Source,
In such least rills from thy Infinity,
As in a broken mirror, parts of Thee
Are seen obscurely. What art Thou entire?—
In Thy unveiled Originality?
In vain imagination plumes her wings,
Such height sublime she may not hope to reach.

O my purged bosom; O my lifted soul;
My bosom purged as with yon waters pure,
And lifted from the mire of selfishness
My soul, till self appear absorbed in God;
Once having seen, once having heard and felt
The almost manifested Deity,
Canst thou again descend to grovelling thoughts?
Canst thou return again as the washed swine
Unto her wallowing? It cannot be,
While memory survives she shall hold up
Before thy view this emblem of thy Lord;
The undying echo of this seven-fold trump
Accompanying thee forevermore
Shall urge thee on to deeds approved of heaven.

DRAMATIC SKETCH.

DRAMATIS PERSONÆ.

CRABBED FARMER, *owner of the grounds where the scene lies.*
WHIMSICAL STUDENT, *seeking recreation.*

SCENE.—*A wood near a stream.*

Enter FARMER *and* STUDENT *from opposite sides.*

Farmer. What are you doing here upon my grounds?
Who may you be?

Student. None other than I seem,
Thus fancy led o'er nature's free domain.
Anon I go to bathe in yonder stream.
Hast ought to object?

Far. Leave, or I'll sue for trespass.
I'll have no bathing on my premises.

Stu. Father, forgive our trespasses; for man
Will sue on at the law, and take his purse;
Nay, take his God-given birthright, liberty.
Hast speculation, clown? Seeing this stream,

Canst thou tell whence it came, and whither goes—
Its ebb and flow—relations numberless?
Know'st thou 'tis but a vein of earth's great body,
Returning laden to the earth's great heart,
Whence it came forth? Know'st thou that mighty heart,
Its tidal pulses—systole, diastole?
Hast thou considered the arterial clouds
Which bear the foodful rains o'er every land,—
The nutrient life-blood of the teeming earth?
Hast traced the capillary veins minute,
Tapping deep wells to fill the hill-side springs,
That feed this circulating stream which is
Articular to the vast living whole,
Upon whose face thou feedest vermin-like?
Dwells logic in thy brain? Are the clouds thine?
Is the great ocean thine?

Far. You say big words
And look so wise to frighten me, perhaps;
But I've seen owls in the woods, and heard them hoot.
The stream is mine. You shall not bathe in it.

Stu. Thou liest utterly. It is God's stream.
He pours it from His mountain urn for all,—
For me to lave my wearied limbs therein.
Meandering, it carries health and joy
To distant lands. Yet thou darest call it thine.
Canst gather it? Canst store it in thy barn?
Thy stream! Hence, or I'll fling thee in thy stream,
And make thee food for the indignant fishes
Which thou wouldst fain forbid to swim thy stream.
Begone, or ere I make thee swallow it;
For with a touch of this magician's wand,
I will transform thee to a monstrous swine,
Thy just shape which thou wearest in thy heart,
And thou shalt wallow in thy stream, and drink,
Yea, drink it as it flows, with thirst unquenched,
While ever and anon thou gruntest "*Mine.*"

Exit CLOWN, *looking back with apprehension.*

Stu. (*solus.*) How He that sitteth in the heavens must smile

To hear earth's little Landlords utter "*Mine!*"
To hear them mouth it in such pompous style.
Appropriation is their highest skill.
They would even reap the stars which God hath sown,
And call the rainbow theirs if it but rest
Its glorious limb on their potato patch.

Written in 1844.

AFTER-THOUGHTS.

I.

O TONGUE-TIED love, too slow, too poor of speech,
 What wealth of meaning hast thou left unsaid:
 What longing looks all blindly left unread
 Until the well-beloved is out of reach!

And though love's intuition lend to each
 A clew whereby he cannot be misled,
 How oft the opportunity is fled
 Ere willing hand can do what heart may teach!

Surcharged regret, thy self-reproach forbear.
 Couldst wish love's every duty fully done,
 No further use for fond affection's care?

On short-lived earth the work is scarce begun:
 And bounteous heaven hath endless days to spare
 For service to thy best-belovèd one.

II.

PARTED! and must I see the face no more
　　Whose smile first wakened longings in my breast,
　　And all through life with constant sunshine blest?
　　But now 'tis hid by heaven's exclusive door.

Nay, say not parted: only gone before
　　To seek the mansion of our final rest,
　　Bespeak a welcome for the coming guest,
　　And then await thee on the wishful shore.

Some duties still amid earth's busy marts;
　　For dear ones still some needful ministry;
　　Then, weary world, receive my last adieu.

With youth renewed, and care-disburdened hearts,
　　Together, hand-in-hand, we'll wander free
　　The fields of light with vistas ever new.

III.

Though veiled from outward sight, thou art more near
    Since envious space hath ceased to intervene,
    And daily cares no longer come between,
    Nor vague alarms distract with idle fear.

Now early hope's fair visions reappear
    Undimmed by dusty time's care-woven screen;
    And I again behold that smile serene
Where truth and trust are mirrored calm and clear.

Thy silent presence speaks in duty's name,
    And leads the way that willing feet must go
    To find again the home from which we came.

And oft to memory's ear in murmurs low
    Thy voice familiar seems to come the same;
    And widowed love the while forgets its woe.

IV.

Not hers the gift to trace from hidden start
    The deep and silent tide-waves in the mind,
    Which overflow in love to humankind;
Of Mercy's Ocean infinite a part.

Spontaneous charity her only art,
    To cheer the sick, the broken heart to bind.
    Love's second-sight infallibly divined
The wants and wishes of the yearning heart.

Whence had this artless soul such happy grace?
    Whence came the wisdom ever to refuse
    The showy blandishments of mere success?

Why seemed she to prefer the lower place?
    Unconsciously she first let others choose,
    Her simple secret self-forgetfulness.

V.

Too late! too late! If only he had known
   The sudden stroke prepared by cruel fate,
   He had not raised the helpless cry "too late,"
With the last chance for reparation flown.

A seasonable word, a gentle tone
   Perhaps had quite removed some crushing weight,
   That quelled at last his uncomplaining mate,
And left him leisure to repent alone.

Procrastination ever waits a day,
   Intending full performance on the morrow,
   When favoring circumstance shall smooth the way.

Thus lavishly the prodigal will borrow,
   And heap up usury he cannot pay,
   Leaving at last a legacy of sorrow.

VI.

It seemed the flowers of her garden knew
  The gentle hand that ministered to them,
  And gave support to every weaker stem.
A withered branch, by her if planted, grew.

To quiet tastes and simple instincts true,
  She chose not, for a queenly diadem,
  Colors that dazzle, like the gaudy gem:
She loved the modest buds of paler hue.

Let friendly hands transplant her favorite flowers
  To deck the precincts of her lowly grave,
  And ever bloom 'neath summer suns and showers.

But think not she is there, a charnel slave.
  She's risen—escaped this prison-house of ours,
  Her spirit safe returned to God who gave.

VII.

If Mary or Martha were her proper name
 Might challenge careful scrutiny to tell;
 Since either character became her well:
 She filled each *rôle* in turn with equal fame.

The ordering of her household free from blame,
 In peace and plenty causing all to dwell,—
 Amid much serving anxious to excel,—
 To Martha's homely virtue proved her claim.

Yet none the less she chose the better part,
 And meekly sat at the Redeemer's feet
 To learn the holy lessons of the heart.

The graduate of earth's best discipline,
 A universal welcome she will meet
 Where'er unselfish love determines kin.

VIII.

From the rank harvest-fields of bitter woe,
    Though faith and patience diligently reap
    Sweet aftermaths of resignation deep,
    Yet still the sigh returns, the tear will flow.

Retracing by-gone paths as lone we go,
    At many a landmark sudden joy will leap,
    Till sudden recollection makes us weep
    For lost delights we never more may know.

Philosophy, aye, thou art very wise,
    With self-renunciation's proverbs trite
    Ready poor erring mortals to advise.

Yet simple nature will assert her right,
    And Heaven shall hear the heart's unbidden cries,
    Though frigid wisdom suffer sore despite.

IX.

It is the quiet Sabbath's twilight eve.
 I seem to clasp thy hand and press thy side
 While musing, in our long life's eventide,
 On by-gone years. What memories they leave!

Oh the lost hours! Could penitence retrieve
 Their opportunities so misapplied!—
 'Tis only *my* regret that thus doth chide:
 Thou ne'er didst cause a kindred heart to grieve.

Oh frequent be thy visits, blessèd shade.
 Yon happy seats will spare thee for a while,
 On such angelic mission sweetly bent.

Thy patient spirit's sympathetic aid
 Shall help me bear my burden, and beguile
 Life's tedious way, or fill it with content.

X.

Still tugging at the heart from yon dim shore
    The tether firmly tied to loved and lost!
    On life's tumultuous ocean tempest-tost
Hope clings to that sure anchor evermore.

But wherefore wait until the voyage is o'er?
    The spirit's viewless track is nowhere crossed
    By time and space. Then count no other cost
Than love to bring the dear one to thy door.

But where lies hid the spirit's trysting-place
    That meddling stranger never may intrude,
    Nor carping care disturb with anxious face?

The secret chambers of the heart include
    An inner shrine, where private prayer finds grace,
    And there love's early vows may be renewed.

XI.

Give me realities, the sceptic said,—
    Things I can see with eye and touch with hand.
    Let visionaries dream of spirit land,
    And grope among the phantoms of the dead.

While yet he spake there grew a formless dread:
    Cold chills crept toward his heart, well-nigh unmanned.
    For ever near a host of spirits stand,
    And when defied a grewsome spell may shed.

Canst trace with outward eye the vivid thought
    Whose flash outstrips the lightning's rapid glance?
    Can solid-seeming earth love's form enclose?

By hand of flesh and blood was love e'er caught?
    Sense shifts the scenes where fleeting shadows dance.
    Behind those scenes behold where substance glows.

XII.

BEREAVEMENT finds no solace but to weep
   Over the wreck of hope's love-freighted vase,
   Keeping long vigils at the trysting-place,
   Till wearied nature falls at last asleep.

Then suddenly from out the darkness leap
   Into full life familiar form and face,
   With outstretched arms to meet the warm embrace;
   And love once more may peaceful Sabbath keep.

O blessèd sleep that weavest happy dreams
   To make amends for sorrow's waking hours,
   How welcome art thou to the wounded breast!

If mimic death can show such bright foregleams,
   What must we hope with after-life's full powers
   In play, mid Edens of eternal rest.

XIII.

Said Prudence: Let us win the wealth to-day
  For future ease; nor spend before we earn.
  Let love be patient; everything in turn;
No time for soft words now, and idle play.

To-morrow, cares of business put away,
  The heart's affairs shall be our chief concern.
  An altar-fire on home's hearth-stone shall burn,
And Love, the priestess, there shall watch and pray.

Day followed night; men waked and wrought and slept.
  Still Prudence plodded on, with steadfast aim,
  No nearer to the goal. Thus while love wept,

O'er-cautious Prudence wronged its own fair name,
  Cheating itself with promises half kept;
  And that delayed to-morrow never came.

XIV.

The things you fancy real may be so.
   Your fondly cherished hopes may bloom in act.
   Such golden promises may well attract,
   But what we have not seen we cannot know.

Enough that's certain meets us as we go.
   The joy of plenty is a present fact;
   Gaunt famine's ghost still haunts us who have lacked;
   But future good or ill what seer can show?

Has the Agnostic no warm heart to feel?
   No eyes but nature's faulty telescopes?
   No ears to hear love's voiceless melodies?

Be still, and finer senses will reveal
   An inner world of unimagined hopes
   Whose bounds are unexplored eternities.

XV.

Patient thou waitest for us there above.
    Death had no power to change thy native worth.
    Thou art the same that lately dwelt on earth
Absorbed in labors of unselfish love.

There runs a rumor that such raptures move
    The souls that revel in their second birth,
    They needs forget a lost companion's dearth.
Believe it not. No true heart can approve.

While hindered in the service she loves best,—
    Devotion to all offices humane,—
    Think you she cares to sit among the blest?

Angelic joys shall woo that heart in vain:
    She cannot sink into eternal rest
    Till she infolds her dearest cares again.

XVI.

How dull and slow we are to apprehend
    The mystery of death! But yesterday
    A guest was with us. Now a clod of clay
Awaits the grave with other clay to blend.

To-morrow we shall look for our lost friend,
    As if bewildered at his long delay;
    Till urgent use resumes its wonted sway.
But can the heart accept this as the end?

Whence springs the hope of immortality?
    Things seen and heard and handled fail to prove
    What the vast future has in store to give.

'Tis the prophetic heart whose faith can see
    That none shall perish who are kin to love,
    And while God lives, His child perforce must live.

XVII.

How fondly, when a fellow Christian dies,
  We feign that all his hapless troubles cease,
  Turmoil exchanged for the perennial peace
Of dwellers in the mansions of the skies.

The Preacher saith: Where the tree falls it lies.
  Of surface stains the soul may wash its fleece
  In Lethe's flood; but ingrained traits increase,
And show their native hue without disguise.

Is death a conjurer who wields a wand
  To change the leopard's spots, the Ethiop's skin?
  A character not earned no power can give.

Manhood dwells here and casts no wish beyond,
  Nor looks abroad for light that shines within;
  Made fit to die by proving fit to live.

XVIII.

The heart still longs whate'er the lips may say.
    Despite Philosophy's heroic air,
    The bosom feels a pang of deep despair
    That words of wisdom never can allay.

Go where he will she still seems far away.
    To wistful eyes that vainly seek her there,
    The landscape's laughing light, however fair
    To others, comes with cold and dismal ray.

O tedious time, when will thy weary task
    Be done, and thy tired slave obtain release,
    That he may swiftly seek the silent shore?

When will dull space remove the envious mask
    That hides from view the inner realms of peace,
    Where he may find the lost, to part no more?

XIX.

Show me the way to heaven, a spirit prayed,
  And wandered wide with a distracted air,
  Like a lost traveller in deep despair,
  Seeking the path from which his feet have strayed:

My daily offerings on her altars laid,
  The church's vows I kept with anxious care,
  Nor did my hand her charities forbear;
Yet now I seem most cruelly betrayed.

Poor wanderer, know that heaven is not a *place*
  That one may enter in and be at rest.
  Earth life alone is bound by time and space.

Heaven dwells within the pure unselfish breast
  That yearns to share the bounteous gifts of grace.
  Where love is, there alone reside the blest.

XX.

Beyond the river, where the wicked cease
   From troubling, and the weary are at rest,
   When safe arrived and quit of life's vain quest,
Claimèst thou a sure reward of perfect peace?

I tell thee, nay. Except with due increase
   Thy talent be returned, no welcome guest
   Shalt thou sit down to feast among the blest.
In outer darkness hope must wait release.

Wouldst thou be perfect? Yield each selfish aim:
   Go follow Christ to Hades' prisoned horde,
   And help Him minister to grim despair.

When all God's prodigals come home to share
   The bounties of a common Father's board,
   Then mayst thou ask thy portion free from blame.

XXI.

Day after day she filled her wonted place
    So quietly; her presence was a thing
    So common, we forgot that time's swift wing
Was hurrying onward, soon to hide that face.

Some plea of business, some delusive chase
    Of phantom fortune, that should quickly bring
    Leisure to bask in home's perennial Spring,
Was ever stealing from our day of grace.

Now she is gone beyond the utmost reach
    Of mortal ken; and past beyond recall
    Are the mistakes the heart would fain unlive.

Could aught restore that gift of gentle speech,
    That smile whose meaning was good will to all,
    What would not fond affection freely give.

XXII.

Another peaceful holy-day is o'er.
  While gazing on the slowly fading west
  At close of each returning day of rest,
  I miss thy quiet presence more and more.

Each day grows lonelier than the day before,
  Each night a deeper sadness is confest.
  Is there no balm to soothe the homesick breast
  Till heaven vouchsafe our union to restore?

Welcome the daily task that may suffice
  To drug remembrance for a moment's space,
  And with a short oblivion cheat the heart.

At every lull in sorrow's storm of sighs
  Hope leaps up toward the joy it would embrace,—
  The joy of meeting never more to part.

XXIII.

As shadows lengthen from the setting sun,
    The eyes of languid labor westward go.
    The kindling glory seems but meant to show
    The weary working-day is almost done.

The things of time and space have now begun
    To lose the spendor of their noontide glow.
    Life's interest flags; its step becomes more slow,
    Not loath to find the race so nearly run.

Beyond the sunset looms another land.
    The bright mirage reveals a peaceful shore
    Inviting wayworn pilgrims to its strand.

Thither our dearest hopes have gone before;
    And side by side with them we soon shall stand,
    Our place of rest secure forever more.

XXIV.

On the world's stage what though the *rôle* of pain
    With tragic mien usurp the part of pleasure;
    Since neither joy nor sorrow forms the measure
Of an immortal spirit's loss and gain?

What though ambition for a time obtain
    Possession of the world, with ample leisure
    To drain its sensuous cup and waste its treasure
In idle pomp? The victory how vain!

World of pure spirit, void of sham, beside
    Thine awful verities, the shameless choice
Of place o'er honor; the unseemly strife

For strict precedence, with unbounded pride,
    How puerile! Man's multitudinous voice
How hushed in presence of eternal life!

XXV.

Days, weeks, months, years are gliding swiftly by.
   Each moment makes the interval more brief
   That forms the gulf between us and our chief
Desire,—to reunite love's broken tie.

The smile of hope succeeds the long-drawn sigh.
   After a weary night of sleepless grief
   The cheering dawn of morning brings relief,
With promise that the day is drawing nigh.

The bane of pleasure that it ends so soon;
   That life is short, its blessings insecure;
   Tinctures our earthly cup with bitterness.

Eternal Goodness, thy divinest boon
   Is certain tenure, love that must endure,
   A good that greater groweth, never less.

XXVI.

To pass away when full of honored years,
    While yet life's holiest works the hands engage,
    And ere the weakness of decrepit age
    Weighs down the heart with anxious cares and fears;

Crowned with the gracious thoughts of loved compeers,
    Whose earnest prayers and ardent hopes presage
    A glorious future on a wider stage;
    Is this a plea to sanction bitter tears?

If nature still must weep, be it for joy
    That grateful tears relieve the swelling breast,—
    Joy that a soul hath shunned the dark decoy

Of worldly lusts, and through the crucial test
    Of fiery trial purged of earth's alloy,
    Hath entered pure upon eternal rest.

XXVII.

No more shall vain regret indulge the wrong
  Of fancying pictures of what might have been,
  Condemning mere mistake as mortal sin,
And unavailing penitence prolong.

Peace to the buried Past. The heart made strong
  In sorrow's patient school of discipline,
  Awaits the welcome signal to begin
To tune anew love's hymeneal song.

Again I see the apparition fair
  That first I saw in the long, long ago,—
  An angel's smile "descending heaven's stair."

Again life's brightest scenes in rapture glow,
  And dainty choice no memories will share
  Save those where harmonies of love o'erflow.

XXVIII.

"There is no death;" though the wan spectre, fear,
   Still haunt our firesides with its evil eye,
   Disturbing peace with the pernicious lie
   That aught can loose the ties which make life dear.

Though human life at times so frail appear,
   'Tis born of God, and therefore cannot die.
   Anon aspiring to its native sky,
   It rends the veil which hides that inner sphere.

Since life is love, it ever must increase;
   Its large desires are never satisfied;
   It craves exhaustless treasures to disburse.

At each new heaven exchanging gifts of peace,
   Its bounteous empire ever grows more wide,
   Till love inherits the whole universe.

THROUGH FOURSCORE'S SPECTACLES.

THE BOAT-RACE—(INTERCOLLEGIATE).

STRIPPED for the race each promptly mans his oar
    And waits the signal for an even start.
    Like arrows from a bow they swiftly dart,
Leaving a foaming wake to mark their score.

They strain each nerve and muscle more and more
    Till strength and skill have fairly done their part.
    The victors reach the goal with panting heart
While beauty's kerchief hails them from the shore.

What training modern colleges afford!
    What eager strife to be the laureate
    In either noble game of manly sport!

The graduate's diploma should record
    A trained athlete, his badge an oar and bat.
    Mere scholarship—leave to the tamer sort.

THE MEET.

The stirring bugle summons to the chase.
    Youth mounts his hunter with ancestral pride,
    And beauty, smiling sweetly at his side,
    Sits her gay palfrey with a queenly grace.

Over the heathery hills at break-neck pace
    The merry hunters follow in reckless ride
    After the panting game that fain would hide
    Its head,—poor struggler in a hopeless race.

With kind papa to find the needful dollar,
    And dear mamma to spend it without measure,
    Their only care to dress in time for dinner;

Beauty and youth may slip hard training's collar,
    And dance through life the pets of idle pleasure.
    Will heaven be strict with good society's sinner?

GOSSIP.

What's in the wind? Who'll tell us something new?
   Although far-fetched, nor easy to believe,
   'Twill serve the purpose of a short reprieve
From drear ennui, that makes one feel so blue.

What though the story be not strictly true?
   Some harmless fiction in the web to weave
   Brightens the color, nor will long deceive;
To-morrow's rumor's sure to change the hue.

Take measure of the gossip's empty head,
   Or in the balance weigh his hollow heart;
   Both are found wanting, shallow, insincere.

To all the best affections wholly dead
   The gossip shares no love, but only fear,
   Deserving victim of his vulgar art.

SHAM ARISTOCRACY—(family, wealth, sanctity).

My great-grandfather was a gentleman.
    With vulgar work his hands were never soiled.
    To serve his daily needs another toiled.
    And I'm my father's father's father's son.

To me, whose wealth a drudging parent won,
    Exclusive doors have oped when rightly oiled,
    At touch of golden wand has pride uncoiled.
    And while the money lasts I yield to none.

"Stand by thyself: I'm holier than thou."
    So spake the Pharisee's self-righteous pride,
    And looked above for heaven's approving smile.

Love surely leads the Trinity; else how
    Could Power and Wisdom patiently abide
    Presumptuous folly's loftiness of style.

THE PRACTICAL MAN.

Be practical if you would soon succeed.
    Wed policy for better or for worse.
    She'll teach you to "put money in your purse;"
And that is being practical indeed.

Though spendthrifts call economy mere greed,
    Be prompt to gather, backward to disburse.
    To usual perquisites be not averse,
And bend to circumstances at your need.

Strict honesty is quite unpractical.
    The business man must not be over-nice;
    More than well pays is serving men for naught.

True policy is strictly tactical.
    Commodity or man each has its price;
    And heaven itself, some fancy, may be bought.

THE GREAT MONEY LENDER.

The money king is lord of other kings.
   His is the hidden power behind the throne
   Which ministers of state are forced to own,
Since he to lagging enterprise lends wings.

To his retreat a threatening war-cloud brings
   The Powers, each to negotiate a loan.
   His aid or let may hasten or postpone
A general crash of sublunary things.

What rare delight, what triumph thus to feel
   Himself the arbiter of fate's decree,
   From whose decision there is no appeal;

Among the nations quite a deity,
   Dispensing fear and favor, woe and weal.
   Make haste, deliver us, O Bellamy.

MODERN TRAVEL.

Travellers do Europe now in sixty days,
   In squads by contract, paying in advance.
   Viewed simply as a question of finance,
   The personally conducted grand tour pays.

Of rare art-treasures, characters, and ways
   Of course one can't note every circumstance,
   Though quick wit takes in much at one swift glance,
   Where leisure pauses long with lingering gaze.

When asked of the peculiar traits of race;
   What new ideas foreign manners teach,
   They tell of cost, naming each petty fee;

And ladies show some lovely bits of lace,
   To prove that travel polishes the speech,
   They let you hear how they pronounce Paris (Par*ee*).

THE BULLY.

SIR, you've insulted me. I'll teach you how
    To act in presence of a personage
    Of my position on the social stage.
    Make an apology right here and now.

The quiet man, abhorrent of a row
    With an obstreperous bully in a rage,
    And thinking only how to disengage
    Himself, says soothing words and makes a bow.

You've seen a rooster strutting; heard him crow.
    Of old triumphant pride its trumpet blew,
    And still fire-eaters thus their bluster show.

When a dog barks, what should a sane man do?
    Simply keep out of reach, and scarce bestow
    A look upon the snarling bugaboo.

THE DUDE.

The dude hath chosen as life's noblest part
    To wear fine clothing without spot or wrinkle;
    Amid the plain-dressed crowd a gem to twinkle,
The consummation of the tailor's art.

How manages the dude to keep so smart,
    As if the clouds might hesitate to sprinkle
    A thing so prim and sleek and free from crinkle?
He gives the business his whole mind and heart.

Compare that novel advertising plan:
    Sandwiched between placards, young laughter's food,
    Note the perambulating show-case man.

Free advertising is by far more shrewd.
    And to this end the thrifty tailor can
    Use for a show-card the unconscious dude.

FICTION.

At every hearth from immemorial time
   The story-teller is a welcome guest.
   His auditors, with never-failing zest,
Drink in the marvellous tale from foreign clime.

Details of daring deed and horrid crime,
   Prodigious feat and unrefining jest,
   Fit to inflame the boy's susceptive breast,
Sell in one volume for a single dime.

To please the children of a larger growth,
   The modern novelist ransacks his brain
   To find a caricature of God's creation.

New forms of woe to invent he's nothing loath,
   As if the actual world lacked real pain,
   And life worth living were pure affectation.

PESSIMISM.

I TOLD you so. What was there to prevent,
   With uncurbed passion rampant from the first,
   Ready at any moment to outburst
In the direction where 'twas closest pent?

Life's a haphazard game of discontent.
   You're always safe to prophesy the worst,
   Where every one with selfishness is curst,
Each pushing for his own aggrandizement.

Thus the poor pessimist, in his pretence
   That wrong and rapine thrive on every hand,
   Condemns himself to make his censure true.

But take him at his word, and no offence
   Could rouse him more. "I'll have you understand,
   Pert fellow, I am quite as good as you."

CRITICISM.

Who is the author? Has he any friends
To back him? None. Then instantly let fly
The keenest shafts of ridicule and sly
Insinuation. A new name pretends
To take the world by storm, and boldly sends
His challenge without leave obtained of high
Authority. Shove the intruder by.
We'll hear no more of him. His meddling ends.

"But have you *read* his book?" Needless delay:
Its drift is obvious at a hasty glance.
We keep set phrases ready for such cases
Without the loss of labor thrown away.
Allow these parvenus the smallest chance,
They'll crowd our favorites from their easy places.

www.ingramcontent.com/pod-product-compliance
Lightning Source LLC
Chambersburg PA
CBHW020148170426
43199CB00010B/933